The price variations and seasonal trends in commodity markets in the early 2000s

Barry Vale

Author's Note

Please note that I wrote the vast majority of this work in 2009, and that it is written accordingly.

I could have gone for a major rewrite, which may have used up weeks of my spare time, and still not have provided me with an international best seller that pays for my retirement (more than delighted to be wrong by the way).

Instead I have just proof read it, done a thorough spell check and added a brief Epilogue.

Contents

Introduction

The main objective of this study is without doubt to provide a comprehensive analysis of the price variations as well as the seasonal trends in the contemporary global commodity markets. Economists have for many years that such price variations not to mention the impact of seasonal trends in commodity markets have actually been consistent features or occurrences within the contemporary global economic system. These price variations and the connected seasonal trends in commodity markets are actually to a large extent measurable, and are indeed frequently measured by economists, commodity or industrial producers, relevant businesses, and perhaps even governments. The international stock markets are also interested in the price variations within commodity markets.

Arguably the over all levels of availability, demand and supply of the most essential or popular commodities has often been regarded as been of very high importance for stimulating, as well as expanding economic development and growth throughout the global economic system. Commodities have the potential to boost economic growth and profits within the global economic system. Alternatively they can be adversely affected instead by recessions and demand downturns within that global economic system itself. This work does not cover how the price variations alongside seasonal trends within the framework of commodity markets has impacted upon the formation of the global economic system over the last five or six centuries. Instead the focus will be directed upon the apparently unusual or unprecedented levels of the price variations besides the seasonal trends in the commodity markets that have taken place within the last ten years or so.

In the last decade or two there has been much discussion within academic, economic, and political cycles alongside media reports concerning the extension of the globalisation process. Examining the fluctuating or consistent levels of price variations and seasonal trends in the modern commodity markets would provide scope for assessing the influence or otherwise it has upon globalisation itself. It is usually argued that in reality that globalisation has a greater impact upon price variations and seasonal trends in commodity markets than those markets have on the process of globalisation (Cleaver, 2002 p. 10).

Globalisation in effect means that the price variations and seasonal trends in relation to the commodity markets depending on whether or not such trends are positive or negative in economic terms can have profound consequences for various actors within the global economic system. As will examined in greater detail these are price variations for goods, products, or services (Thrift, 2005 p. 5). Price variations that can be shaped by such actors within the global economic system as well as the seasonal trends within commodity markets, which might not be so controllable by individuals, businesses, and also national governments. Price variations for commodities are also often linked to the strengths or the weaknesses of share values upon the international stock markets (Bannock, Baxter, & Davis, 2003 p. 60).

The ability not to mention the capacity to transport a wide selection of goods, products, and services has an impact upon the price variations and also the seasonal trends in commodity markets besides possibly being connected to the development and the expansion of the globalisation process. High demand for, goods, products, and less frequently services when their availability is restricted logically leads to higher prices perhaps irrespectively of other price variations and seasonal trends in commodity markets. Logically in the reverse situation of the goods, products, and raw materials being produced in large quantities but demand is low then the prices should decrease regardless of any seasonal variations or other trends within the contemporary commodity markets (Cleaver, 2002 p. 10).

Theoretically if there was no substantial intervention within the global economic system then all the price variations and also the seasonal trends in the contemporary commodity markets would be solely determined by the over all levels of demand and supply. However other factors besides demand and supply levels are able to influence, or indeed alter the price variations and seasonal trends generally experienced in the commodity markets in the last decade (Cleaver, 2002 p. 10). These other factors that affect the price variations aside from the seasonal trends in the commodity markets of the global economic system will be examined in the subsequent chapters.

Chapter One - the definition and explanation of the price variations and seasonal trends within the commodity markets

To begin with there are two basic definitions of the word commodity. After all to start to understand price variations and seasonal trends in commodity markets the concepts relating to the sale or production of commodities needs to be explained (Begg, Fischer, & Dornbusch, 2005 p. 627).

Firstly, "in economic theory a commodity is a tangible good or service resulting from the process of production" (Bannock, Baxter, & Davis, 2003 p. 60).

Secondly a commodity is also "a primary product e. g. coffee, copper, cotton, wool, rubber and tin" (Bannock, Baxter, & Davis, 2003 p. 60).

To put it in the most basic terms then commodities are therefore goods, products, and services, which are sold by producers. These goods and products are then brought by other producers, as well as consumers in order to be made into products of a greater value. These will be goods that are either to be sold on for higher prices, or for purchased for personal consumption. Generally economists argue that the price variations for any commodity are related to the balance between the total demand for that good in relation to the number of individual units of it that can be supplied. Whenever traders or companies buy commodities to sell on for profit, or to invest in the businesses that sell them they are always taking risks. Involvement in global commodity markets can just as easily go wrong as it can go right. Commodity markets are at risk from high inflation wiping out the real value of the goods invested in, low demand for those goods, or the commodities being of a low quality (Grauer & Litzenberger, 1979 p. 70).

For the majority of commodities the price will go down if supply matches demand, whilst prices should increase when supply fails to keep up with over all demand (Ison, 2000 p. 34). Price variations and seasonal trends in commodity markets are nearly always affected by the relationship between demand and supply for each type of commodity as well as being capable of affecting such activity (Bannock, Baxter, & Davis, 2003 p.60). Seasonal trends and over all levels of demand is not the only factors that can be beneficial or harmful to commodity prices. Commodity prices are more likely to predictable and less varied if international currencies, especially the American dollar have a stable value and exchange rate (Gilpin, 1987 p. 74).

Commodity markets were originally referred to as commodity exchanges due to them being physical auction or market places where commodities were actually brought, sold, or exchanged for goods, products, as well as services of a similar or well – recognised value (Bannock, Baxter, & Davis, 2003 p.60). The traditional commodity markets were slow to buy, exchange, or sell commodities although before the advent of cars, trains, and planes it could take weeks to transport goods, raw materials, and products across the globe (Ison, 2000 p. 34). The days when small parts of each consignment or batch of commodities, goods, or materials had to inspected and shown by their respective sellers to all interested potential buyers are now long gone (Bannock, Baxter, & Davis, 2003 p.60). Instead commodities are usually brought and also sold by both their buyers and their sellers. Usually the only people or groups that will have seen or examined the quality of the commodities being transported to be sold are the primary commodity producers themselves (Bannock, Baxter, & Davis, 2003 p.287).

The introduction of computerised commodity and stock markets from the 1980s and the advent of the Internet now mean that commodities can effectively be brought and sold to anyone or any business across the globe twenty - four hours a day every single day of the year. Individual consumers and businesses are now able to take advantage of the opportunities to buy or to sell commodities and services online cutting out the requirement for completing transactions in store on the high street. Online trading can allow consumers to take advantage of bargains whilst reducing overhead costs for companies. The last decade has therefore experienced a great increase in the volumes of commodities, goods, and services brought and sold on the Internet (Thrift, 2005 p. 182). Whether or not commodity markets are computerised business confidence can make all the difference between boom and bust. Trade restrictions, a loss of stock market, or consumer confidence, or even political turmoil can all act to undermine the contemporary economic system (Gilpin, 1987 p. 77).

Merchants and traders involved in the buying and selling of commodity use the contemporary computerised commodity exchanges, in order to buy commodities in bulk, in an attempt to avoid the largest price variations within the commodity market. They still have the same old disadvantage of not knowing how risky their commodity investments are (Grauer & Litzenberger, 1979 p. 70). Online commodity markets have the advantage that transactions can be carried out with greater speed at anytime and from any place (Thrift, 2005 p.182). Computerised commodity markets are also a factor in reflecting the price variations and seasonal trends that occur in the present day global economic system (Ison, 2000 p. 5).

In many respects concentrating the locations for the commodity markets especially spot markets can be advantageous for both producers, as well as the potential buyers and also the consumers of the goods sold at these markets (Thrift, 2005 p. 182). Buying or selling commodities and specialised spot markets allows buyers, producers and also sellers to save money by reducing overheads as well as reducing the prices of the items being sold (Bannock, Baxter, & Davis, 2003 p. 60). Slade and Thille have argued that commodity prices can vary depending on whether or not the structure of each specific industry is effectively managed and works properly. Companies that are effectively organised are less likely to be unfavourably treated by seasonal trends and changes in demand (Slade and Thille, 2004 p. 3).

Producers appreciate lower selling costs whilst consumers of course will be keen to buy the commodities that they either need or want at lower prices. Commodities are available to be brought and sold as many different kinds of goods, products, and also services (Bannock, Baxter, & Davis, 2003 p. 60). Some commodities are more vulnerable to price variations and also seasonal trends than other goods, materials or products are (Begg, Fischer, & Dornbusch, 2005 p. 627). For instance seasonal trends are most likely to affect the availability of perishable agrarian products such as fresh fruit, fresh vegetables, and even flowers as these types of commodities that need to be processed, packaged, brought, sold, and also delivered as soon as possible (Thrift, 2005 p. 8). The price variations of agrarian produced foods and commodities could be effected, as much by changes in consumer tastes or the decisions of major retailers and supermarkets about what types of goods they want to sell in their stores. For instance the demand for sugar in North America and Western Europe to be used to sweeten drinks and food has continued to decline (Begg, Fischer, & Dornbusch, 2005 p. 627, Cleaver, 2002 p. 10).

These perishable agrarian produced commodities can generally only be grown at certain times or seasons of the year as well as in certain parts of the world (Bannock, Baxter, & Davis, 2003 p.287). Some of these agricultural and horticultural commodities could be grown out of their naturally occurring seasons in different parts of the world if producers are willing to put extra efforts into growing and processing these goods, and consumers are prepared to pay higher prices (Cleaver, 2002 p. 10). However the requirement for increased energy and transportation costs could that the final goods are excessively priced when they are put up for sale in their respective commodity markets (Begg, Fischer, & Dornbusch, 2005 p. 627).

Perishable fresh fruits alongside fresh vegetables could be particularly at high risks from poor harvests that are caused by not enough rain fall, too much rain resulting in flooded crops, or by hard frost and heavy snow fall during severe winters (Bannock, Baxter, & Davis, 2003 p. 60). The price variations as well as the seasonal trends in the agrarian commodity markets are dependent upon good weather to avoid food shortages and very high prices. Droughts, floods, and severe winters have the capability to restrict or even completely destroy crop - based commodities with little or no warning at all (Begg, Fischer, & Dornbusch, 2005 p. 627). In 2007 poor wheat harvests meant that the average price for a bushel of wheat was around $10 in 2008. Extra crop planting in 2008 has meant that prices have not gone back to their previous levels.

The producers of agrarian and horticultural commodities in the developing countries especially those in sub – Saharan Africa are the nation states most generally expected to suffer from severe weather conditions that could wipe out their entire crops. It is not just the developing countries that could experience price variations and seasonal trends in commodity markets due to unexpected weather patterns (Begg, Fischer, & Dornbusch, 2005 p. 627). In the contemporary world therefore adverse weather conditions can when unexpectedly experienced in any part of the globe, and more extreme conditions have been noted in the last decade or so (Thrift, 2005 p. 182).

Poor harvests can adversely affect commodity producers, farmers, businesses, and consumers alike. In the worst cases severe food shortages can result in the onset of famines, with there been virtually no food commodities left to be sold. In such situations what little quantities of food supplies are left will become far too expensive for most ordinary people to afford (Ison, 2000 p. 35). Drastically reduced food crop yields should of course push up agricultural and horticultural commodity prices up over the short – term. However shortages over the long – term will probably have severe detrimental consequences for the producers, consumers, and also the national governments of some of the world's poorest and economically least well – developed nation states (Begg, Fischer, & Dornbusch, 2005 p. 627).

Upward moving commodity price variations caused by bad weather and unfavourable seasonal trends in commodity markets are exactly what these already poor nation states do not need for their present and future economic development (Begg, Fischer, & Dornbusch, 2005 p. 627). In the most extreme price variations caused by droughts or floods rather than seasonal trends in commodity markets the smallest – scale commodity producers, businesses, as well as national governments (due to declining revenues derived from lower levels of export duties) will make less money over all. Less money will be made as a direct or occasionally an indirect result of crop yields falling. Such situations again demonstrate the relationship between demand and supply when it comes to understand price variations in contemporary commodity markets (Ison, 2000 p. 32). It is the consumers that could be doubly affected by lower agricultural and horticultural crop output as they have to pay more for their staple food supplies, and also potentially having less to eat, or less variety of food to consume within their diet (Begg, Fischer, & Dornbusch, 2005 p. 627).

If the worst -case scenarios and predictions about the climatic changes caused by global warming are proven to be well-founded then the potential for price variations caused by adverse weather conditions and not just seasonal trends should become increasingly apparent in the commodity markets. That can be regarded as yet another example of potential price variations being caused by demand for commodities outstripping the supply of each particular good (Ison, 2000 p. 36).

Global warming and high human population growth also entails that water both for drinking

purposes and the irrigation of agricultural crops is thus becoming increasingly scarce, whilst

remaining vital for the viable growth of commodities as well as staple food supplies (Bannock,

Baxter, & Davis, 2003 p.60). In recent years the price variations and seasonal trends in

agricultural and food commodity markets has tended to increase due to the reduced food

production levels of the most popular and consumed staple food crops such as maize, rice, and

wheat (Begg, Fischer, & Dornbusch, 2005 p. 627).

The widely reported onset of the global credit crunch in 2007 and its spread throughout 2008

may or may not mean that the bulk of food commodity prices could fall due to declining levels of

over all demand for them (Klein, 2007 p. 455). Credit crunch induced price variations could

easily make the normally experienced seasonal trends less influential in the commodity markets.

People might have the desire or need to eat the same volume of food that they did before the

credit crunch began yet lack the financial means to do just that. Decreased demand across the

globe will probably be as harmful to the revenues of agrarian commodity producers as the over –

production of their crops, and could quite possibly be worse (Bromley, Mackintosh, Brown, and

Wuyts, 2004 p. 14). Bumper harvest yields for agricultural and food crops can be highly

damaging for the income levels of the commodity producers as well as the businesses that sell

these goods to consumers. Whenever there are bumper agricultural commodity crops it should

be the consumers that are able to benefit from lower food prices in the shops or on the high street

(Begg, Fischer, & Dornbusch, 2005 p. 627).

Logically enough poor harvests lead to strongly upward price variations as well as seasonal

trends in commodity markets, which conversely raise the income that producers and businesses make from selling agricultural and horticultural commodities (Ison, 2000 p. 35). Price variations

can be controlled and seasonal trends made less influential in the commodity markets if they are

altered or managed by producers and businesses. In fact commodity producers and businesses

selling goods and services can increase their income levels from commodity sales by recreating

conditions of scarcity (Begg, Fischer, & Dornbusch, 2005 p. 627).

Commodity producers, whether they are producing perishable food produce as well as raw

materials such as copper, tin and crude oil can make greater profits from higher prices by

restricting supplies going into the global economic system (Ison, 2000 p. 36). In the last decade

commodity producers of goods such as coffee and tin have attempted to recreate the production

quotas implemented with relative success by the major oil producing countries of the

Organisation of Petroleum Exporting Countries (OPEC). The systematic fixing, restricting and

stabilising the price of commodities is arguably to the advantage of the main producers if they

are capable of ensuring that all production quotas are adhered to. Such elimination of price

variation could also be good for businesses whilst not being especially beneficial for individual

consumers (Begg, Fischer, & Dornbusch, 2005 p. 627).

Production quotas are rendered next to useless if any of the commodity producers produce more

than their quota in order to take advantage of higher prices in the relevant commodity markets

(Bannock, Baxter, & Davis, 2003 p.287). In the last decade or so it has mostly been primary

commodity producers within the developing countries that have attempted to increase their

profits and revenues via the introduction or extension of production quotas for commodities and

goods that they produce (Klein, 2007 p. 69). To a large extent these measures have not been too

successful. However the extension of fair trade schemes that pay commodity producers a higher

price for their commodities such as tea and coffee have been noticeable in the last ten years.

Supermarkets and coffee shop chains as well as fast food chains now generally sell fair trade products in their outlets (Begg, Fischer, & Dornbusch, 2005 p. 627).

With the notable exception of crude oil and natural gas price variations and seasonal trends in the commodity market can have considerable impact upon the demand and supply of goods. The demand for natural gas is more prone to seasonal trends in use if not always prices as individuals and businesses use greater quantities of it during winter for heating purposes (Ison, 2000 p. 37). Non-perishable commodities are less subject to the price variations brought about by seasonal trends in commodity markets. Droughts and floods have the capacity to wipe out or drastically cut the production of agrarian commodities, yet should not have any effect or influence over the production levels or the costs of non-perishable goods (Begg, Fischer, & Dornbusch, 2005 p. 627).

Although seasonal trends should not aversely or favourably affect the value and price of non-perishable commodities altering levels of demand caused by economic booms or recessions especially in North America, Western Europe and Japan can quickly affect commodity producers in the developing countries (Klein, 2007 p. 79). Economic booms tend to markedly increase the demand for the commodities such as copper that are used in the information technology based industries as well as in the construction or housing industries. However, during economic downturns or recession, demand for copper will fall substantially. Early indications are that the credit crunch, which commenced in 2007, and has severely affected North America, Western Europe, and Asia, will become the worst global economic recession since the Wall Street Crash of 1929, which set off the Great Depression. In many respects the credit crunch was to the largest extent inadvertently caused by the reckless lending of many leading banks and financial institutions to businesses and individuals that were in poor positions to be able to pay back these loans (Cleaver, 2002 p. 10). Until the middle years of the 1980s economists nearly all agreed that in the capitalist global economic system it was over all levels of demand and the value of every commodity in relation to the American dollar that was most important. For when combined they determined its openness to price variations within the international commodity markets (Chaudari, 2001 p. 531).

It can be soundly argued that the presently ongoing credit crunch has been able to have devastating consequences due to the process of globalisation making the commodity markets and financial markets increasingly inter linked to each other within the global economic system (Thrift, 2005 p. 5). To a very large extent the reckless lending of loans to individual borrowers and businesses that were high risks caused the credit crunch. These people and businesses were risks in terms of their inability to repay their loans to the banks and other financial institutions that had lent them the money in the first place (Bannock, Baxter, & Davis, 2003 p.287). In the contemporary global economic system a great deal of the consumption of commodities by individual consumers and business is funded by credit rather than cash payments from earnings or savings (Begg, Fischer, & Dornbusch, 2005 p. 627).

Commodities are generally purchased through credit payments, thus if credit becomes more expensive to repay, or if banks are incapable of supplying high levels of lending, then it would logically have the knock on effect of decreasing the demand for commodities (Klein, 2007 p.342). The credit crunch, a severe recession by another name, just like previous global recessions has reduced the amount of credit available to be lent to individuals and businesses, which in return leads to falling commodity sales over all as well as eventually leading to increased levels of unemployment. In turn those people that lose their jobs are not able to spend as much on commodities, services and other leisure items leading to even further decrease in demand levels and theoretically at least prices (Begg, Fischer, & Dornbusch, 2005 p. 627).

The credit crunch has been spread further and wider due to contemporary advanced it and extended modern media coverage have it generally contended meant the fear of worldwide recession has spread across the globe. Fear when combined with the huge high – risk loans made by banks and other financial institutions in turn adding to the loss of business and consumer confidence that has been dubbed the credit crunch rather than been referred to as a global economic recession. The consumers in North America, Europe and Asia appear to be reducing their consumption of goods, products and services drastically in ways that are not covered by the average impacts of price variations and seasonal trends that operate within commodity markets operating in the contemporary global economic system. If the worst predictions about the credit crunch prove to be highly accurate it will have serious and perhaps even long – term consequences for commodity markets. The credit crunch will lead to large numbers of primary commodity producers, businesses, and consumers suffering heavy financial losses, going into liquidation or become insolvent or bankrupt (Bannock, Baxter, & Davis, 2003 p.287).

Crude oil as well as other gas or petroleum based products are commodities that are frequently subject to wide - ranging price variations without in any significant way being affected by seasonal trends in the international commodity markets (Bannock, Baxter, & Davis, 2003 p.287). Over the years the worldwide demand for crude oil, natural gas, and petroleum based products has proved to be realistic to be inelastic with depressions, recessions, or indeed the present credit crunch seemingly having very little impact on price variations or actual production levels (Begg, Fischer, & Dornbusch, 2005 p. 627).

Over the long - term the global demand for crude oil and its related by products will eventually far outstrip actual supply levels as all the world's gas and oil reserves near exhaustion (Bannock,

Baxter, & Davis, 2003 p.287). Crude oil and natural gas price variations are often heavily

dependent upon the production quota levels set by OPEC as well as whether or not its member

states stick to those production limits (Begg, Fischer, & Dornbusch, 2005 p. 627). OPEC sets

production quota levels in order to maximise the over all revenue from gas, oil, and petrol sales.

Given the importance of crude oil and its other by products to the contemporary global economic

system any substantial price variations can cause marked alterations for the demand as well as

the price level of many other goods in their respective commodity markets (Bannock, Baxter, &

Davis, 2003 p.287).

Not only can reduced crude oil production quotas drastically increase the price of that essential

commodity for instance in the oil crisis of 1973, but fears about the security of such supplies can

also push up global prices. Price increases that often happen whether or not they are realistic

concerns (Begg, Fischer, & Dornbusch, 2005 p. 627). The success of OPEC demonstrates that

national governments and non-governmental organisations have the capacity to alter the

commodity markets and therefore the global economic system when it suits them to do so

(Frieden and Lake, 2000 p. 2).

The national economies of the majority of the Middle Eastern countries, North African countries,

and to a lesser extent those of the West Indies / Caribbean and Sub-Saharan Africa are highly

dependent upon specialised exports. In that respect the actions of OPEC in fixing oil prices is

entirely logical (Dehn, 2000 p. 10). The developing countries and to a large extent the developed

states within the Middle East would prefer stable commodity prices, though at differing levels.

After all uncertainty over commodity prices can be particularly serious for such countries to

contend with. Extensive price variations can reduce the capacity of developing countries to pay

off their substantial economic debts (Dehn, 2000 p.1).

Early indicators are that the credit crunch will lower food commodity prices, as people will spend less money on such products due to reduced personal budgets. Non-perishable and non oil / petroleum commodities in the last ten years have seen price variations that have more to do with economic cycles of boom and bust than seasonal trends when sold in commodity markets (Bannock, Baxter, & Davis, 2003 p.287). For much of the 2000s many countries within North America, Western Europe and Asia were apparently experiencing an economic boom, which had a knock on effect on the price of commodities (Bannock, Baxter, & Davis, 2003 p.287). Not all commodities went up in price, yet there was a strong demand for metals like copper, which is a highly adaptable and useful material, especially in the construction as well as the electronic industries (Smith, 2003 p. 10). In previous global recessions demand for copper and other high value commodities has dropped as the industries that would make the most use out of them have usually been badly affected by falling demand for their own goods, products and services (Bannock, Baxter, & Davis, 2003 p.287). Other commodities such as diamonds, gold and silver have demonstrated a remarkable capacity to retain high value, high prices, and high levels of demand irrespective of global economic booms or worldwide economic recessions (Bannock, Baxter, & Davis, 2003 p.287).

Chapter Two – Literature Review of sources relating to price variations and seasonal trends in commodity markets

The Penguin Dictionary of Economics by Bannock, Baxter, & Davis, was used to provide background information and definitions concerning price variations and seasonal trends in commodity markets.

Economics 8th edition by Begg, Fischer, & Dornbusch published in 2005 was used in relation to gaining information about the price variations and also the seasonal trends in contemporary commodity markets. Specifically the book by Begg, Fischer, & Dornbusch was useful for information concerning agrarian commodities as well as assisting with analysis and explanation of production quotas. The brief section in Begg, Fischer, & Dornbusch concerning OPEC and the inelastic demand levels for crude oil and petroleum was particularly useful. To an extent OPEC is the one organisation that has come closest to controlling price variations and seasonal trends within commodity markets to suit the interests of its member countries.

Bromley, Mackintosh, Brown, and Wuyts (2004) - Making the International: Economic Interdependence and Political Order, was used for information about globalisation.

Cleaver's, Understanding the World Economy was useful for information about globalisation and the contemporary global economic system.

The article Commodity Price Uncertainty in Developing Countries by Dehn focuses upon the greater dependence of developing countries upon stable commodity markets.

Fisk's The Great War for Civilisation – the conquest of the Middle East, was used in relation to crude oil prices and impact of stability or otherwise in the Middle East.

Frieden and Lake's International Political Economy – Perspectives on Global Power and Wealth was useful reference with regard to state and non-governmental organisation intervention in the commodity markets.

The Political Economy of International Relations by Gilpin was helpful for discussing the effect of currency stability upon price variations.

The journal article by Grauer & Litzenberger was used in order to understand the risks involved with trading or investing in the global commodity markets.

The book Frameworks – Economics (3rd edition) by Stephen Ison assists in the explaining of price variations and seasonal trends in commodity markets by describing the theoretical aspects of demand and supply. The book provides information concerning the link between demand and supply provides ways to explain how the price variations as well as the seasonal trends in commodity markets come about or occur.

 Naomi Klein's book 'The Shock Doctrine – The Rise of Disaster Capitalism, first published in 2007 is particularly for its information concerning globalisation and the importance of crude oil to the global economic system. Especially helpful for explaining the importance of the oil industry in relation to worldwide price variations and seasonal trends in commodity markets.

The journal article 'Long run prices of primary commodities and oil prices' by Kausik Chaudari, in the 2001 copy of Applied Economics suggested ways of studying price variations. This article seeks to suggest alternative ways of understanding the price variations and the seasonal trends experienced in modern day commodity markets

Siebert, The World Economy useful for general information about the world economy and development issues.

The article Commodity Spot Prices: An Exploratory Assessment of Market Structure and Forward Trading Effects by Slade and Thille touched upon effective companies being able to avoid the worst consequences of price variations.

David Smith's 'Free Lunch –Easily Digestible Economics, Served on a plate, was useful for background information on globalisation and stock markets.

Commodity of the month: Wheat, The Spectator article by Laura Staples examines the increase in wheat prices caused by the drop in global production in 2007 caused by poor harvests.

Knowing Capitalism by Nigel Thrift was used to find out about the roles that the process of globalisation and modern technology has played in promoting or restricting price variations and affecting the influence of seasonal trends in modern day commodity markets. Thrift mentioned the affect that modern computers and information technology is having, or potentially could have in relation to the price variations and seasonal trends in commodity markets.

Todd's After the Empire – the breakdown of the American Order was referenced to explain how globalisation was a process promoted by the United States even as its economic position declined in relation to other countries.

Chapter Three - Method and methodology for analysing and explaining price variations and seasonal trends in commodity markets

This work will focus on the current price variations in the commodity markets compared to the last decade or so. The information and research gathered would had to be factual and must be analysed into implications and reasons why there have been these variations. It needs to be discussed in detail of the current economic crisis in the world economy and the influences sustained by the brokers and speculators and traders in the commodity markets. There needs to be detailed mathematical analysis on the current commodity markets and the price variations and its seasonal trends. Statistical data collected must be referenced, state the period, and its purpose. It should also test the market efficiency and market anomalies in the commodities industry.

The data gathered and used in the other parts of this study is included in order to allow an effective evaluation of the causes as well as the consequences of price variations and seasonal trends within the commodity markets. Such factors include over all levels of demand and supply, attempts to control supply, and the effects of unpredicted events and trends. Data and figures that are relevant for an effective analysis of price variations and seasonal trends in the contemporary commodity markets were obtained from various academic and economics text books, as well as journals and newspaper articles.

Chapter Four – overview of price variations and the seasonal trends in the commodity markets in the last decade

Over the last decade or so there have undoubtedly been price variations and seasonal trends in commodity markets within the global economic system (Thrift, 2005 p.181). The actual or potential causes of these price variations and seasonal trends in contemporary commodity markets were discussed in Chapter One, this chapter examines whether these potential causes of price variations and seasonal trends in the commodity markets are demonstrated in reality itself (Klein, 2007 p. 69). It has been argued or frequently assumed that some commodities and goods have a greater over all propensity to be beneficially or alternatively adversely affected by the price variations and also the seasonal trends in the commodity markets that do actually take place (Bannock, Baxter, & Davis, 2003 p.60). Price variations and seasonal trends are often linked together in commodity markets although changing price levels are not always determined by seasonal trends. For instance those commodities produced and sold by companies listed on the major stock markets can have price variations primarily caused by fluctuations in the worth of stocks and shares (Begg, Fischer, & Dornbusch, 2005 p. 627).

In many respects it is the low value mainly agrarian commodities that are obviously the most prone to the inconsistent vagaries of the weather, strongly influencing any price variations and also reflecting seasonal trends in the commodity markets (Bromley, Mackintosh, Brown, and Wuyts, 2004 p. 14). The price variations largely caused by the seasonal trends can make a great deal of difference to the prices paid by the consumers and also profits for the commodity producers and the food retailers within the contemporary commodity markets (Bannock, Baxter,

& Davis, 2003 p.60).

Chapter Five - Findings concerning the price variations and seasonal trends in the commodity markets within the contemporary global economic system

In recent years there were global shortages of staple food crops including rice that has led to markedly increasing price variations that are arguably above and beyond the price fluctuations that can be expected from the normal seasonal trends in the commodity markets (Begg, Fischer, & Dornbusch, 2005 p. 627). It has been a combination of poor harvests and the extra food requirements of rising populations (especially but not exclusively in the developing countries, which have led to increased over all levels of demand for agricultural and horticultural commodities. Extra global demand for food commodities is a long – term cause of the price variations across the world where as seasonal trends are generally short – term causes of price fluctuations within the contemporary commodity markets (Thrift, 2005 p. 17).

The 2000s has undoubtedly been a decade that has experienced previously unprecedented price levels for crude oil and all its related by products, in other words mainly increasing price variations irrespective of the seasonal trends in the present day commodity markets (Bannock, Baxter, & Davis, 2003 p.287). The surge in global crude oil and petroleum prices had arguably mainly non-–economic reasons with the noticeably increased levels of insecurity predominantly caused by the 9 / 11 attacks on the United States and the subsequent decision of the Bush administration to invade Iraq (Klein, 2007 p. 11).

Political decisions by the American government in this particular case influenced the leading commodity price variations rather more than seasonal trends in the commodity markets did, with the invasion of Iraq leading to nervousness in the leading stock markets as well as the main commodity markets. As Iraq is one of the world's largest producers of crude oil the increased tension in 2002 and 2003 based upon the prospects of a United States led invasion prompted the vast rise in oil prices experienced over the next five or six years (Klein, 2007 p. 314).

Previously similar rapid crude oil price increases had set off global economic slowdowns and recessions. For example drastic crude oil price variation way beyond seasonal trends in the commodity markets happened in late 1973 after the Yom Kippur War. Further economic recession resulted from further crude oil price variation in the period between 1979 and 1986 as a consequence of the instability in the Middle East caused by the Iranian Revolution and then the onset of the Iran – Iraq War (Todd, 2002 p. 69). However economists did not predict this turmoil at the time unlike more mundane and predictable seasonal trends in the commodity markets (Bannock, Baxter, & Davis, 2003 p.287).

The crude oil and the petroleum price rises and variations despite been more considerably more important than seasonal trends in the commodity markets did not immediately set off a worldwide recession. In effect the sharp crude oil price variations after 2002 whilst effecting the commodity markets did not cause undue alarm or panic in the main international stock markets. Global recession did not take place in 2002 arguably due to the relatively easy availability of bank credits as well as loans for individuals, businesses, not to mention national governments. With hindsight it was carelessly given credit, banks loans, and electronically spent money were behaving like the main global commodities that were actually keeping the contemporary global economic system going in the early and the middle years of the 2000s (Fisk, 2006 p. 1087). The price variations and also the seasonal trends inside the contemporary commodity markets during the last decade were not as economically healthy as many might have expected. Also to a

large extent the easy availability of bank credit and unparalleled sums of loans kept the world

economy despite the commodity market price of crude oil breaking the $100 a barrel for the first

time in 2007 (Klein, 2007 p. 341).

 In many parts of the world national economies were apparently in good shape up to the middle

of the 2000s with consumers borrowing excessive amounts of credit (Thrift, 2005 p. 15).

Companies and consumers were able to do so due to banks and financial institutions seemingly

lending unwise loans out at will, whilst leading companies were making sound if not always

impressive levels of profit (Klein, 2007 p. 455). The international stock markets, the media,

consumers, and companies and the majority of national governments at this stage were unaware

of the unstable situation that the global economic system was actually in. Examinations of the

price variations and seasonal trends in commodity markets in the middle of the 2000s were

generally regarded as demonstrating that there was anything drastically within the global

economy (Begg, Fischer, & Dornbusch, 2005 p. 627).

The period of modest price variations and mainly insignificant seasonal trends in commodity

markets were effectively ended after 2002, with high consumption and borrowing rates

disguising the risks of a debt crisis and the potential for global recession (Begg, Fischer, &

Dornbusch, 2005 p. 627). The serious and not always noticed problem was that the high rates of

commodity consumption by consumers as well as the turnover and profits of companies were

heavily reliant upon unsustainable high levels of borrowing and unwise bank loans (Klein, 2007

p.79). The international stock markets were more interested in overvaluing the value of stocks

and shares for the majority of the last decade instead of realising that things were about to go

wrong in the most economically disastrous fashion since 1929. The price variations and seasonal trends in commodity markets in the years before the onset of the credit crunch did not appear untoward despite the higher crude oil prices caused by instability in the Middle East (Klein, 2007 p.313).

The affects of record high commodity market prices for crude oil was not adverse or detrimental for everybody with the main oil producing countries, or at the very least their national governments receiving substantially increased revenues. The major oil companies such as British Petroleum (BP) and Royal Dutch Shell throughout the last decade or so have made very substantial profits due to the unheard of global price of crude oil and all of its related by products (Klein, 2007 p.341). Indeed because of the way BP and Royal Dutch Shell store around three months worth of gas, petrol, and oil they are in very strong positions to use the price variations and seasonal trends in the commodity markets to their commercial advantage (Klein, 2007 p. 341).

The majority of businesses have attempted to offset the increasingly heavy fuel and energy costs they have been faced with by raising the prices of the goods, products, and also the services, which they sell (Siebert, 2002 p. 180). Prior to the onset of the credit crunch the majority of companies were able to increase the prices of their goods, products and services without driving too many of their customers away from them (Klein, 2007 p. 313). Generally it was the ordinary consumers that suffered the most for the price variation and to a lesser extent the seasonal trends in the commodity markets caused either directly or indirectly by the high global prices for crude oil. The majority of studies into price variations within international commodity markets show that the link between crude oil price changes and price alterations in other primary commodities are very strong. When crude oil goes up in price nearly every other commodity goes up in price as well (Chaudari, 2001 p. 534)

A combination of high crude oil prices and relatively strong economic growth rates were conducive to higher over all price variations in the majority of commodity markets, at least in the early years of the 2000s. Higher crude oil prices and economic growth rates increased inflationary pressures over all within the global economic system. To a large extent inflation rises were a logical consequence of the increased energy and transportation costs with the oil price hikes and the increased scarcity of some commodities in a period of stronger economic growth. The majority of commodities of course need to use energy to be produced before fuel is used to transport these goods to the commodity markets in which they are to be sold in. Therefore raised crude oil and petroleum costs result in commodity producers and businesses increasing the costs of their goods to pay higher fuel bills.

Price variations were also on an upward move in most of the international commodity markets as demand for the most popular and useful commodities generally went up. The upward movements in the price variations whether or not influenced by seasonal trends came to a largely unexpected and also unpredicted slump in global levels of demand quickly described by the media, governments and economists as the credit crunch (Klein, 2007 p. 79). Although a global economic recession had not been caused by rocketing oil prices price variations inside commodity markets started to decline. Oil prices are in many ways the most important single influence upon the price variations of all other primary goods, commodities and services. Levels of demand, stock market confidence (or lack of it), currency stability, and security issues can also have an impact as well. Finally the climate can have an impact upon food commodities, though transport costs are more important than seasonal trends (Chaudari, 2001 p. 535).

A decline due to the consequences of banks and financial institutions reeling in the wake of the sub-prime mortgages crisis in the United States and the collapse of the Northern Rock bank in the United Kingdom. The unsustainable levels of bad debt especially in North America and

Western Europe directly started the credit crunch leading to a sharp economic recession in most

if not all parts of the world.

Chapter Six – conclusions concerning the price variations and the seasonal trends in the commodity markets in the last decade

Price variations and seasonal trends are often linked together in commodity markets although changing price levels are not always determined by seasonal trends. For instance those commodities produced and sold by companies listed on the major stock markets can have price variations primarily caused by fluctuations in the worth of stocks and shares.

To conclude the last decade or so has seen some wide – ranging price variations not to mention drastic changes within the global economic system. These changes in the global economic system were assisted via the introduction of computerised commodity and stock markets from the 1980s. After that the emergence of the Internet now allows commodities to be effectively brought as well as sold to anyone or any business across the globe twenty - four hours a day every single day of the year. Individual consumers and businesses are now able to take advantage of the opportunities to buy or to sell commodities and services online cutting out the requirement for completing transactions in store on the high street. Online trading can allow consumers to take advantage of bargains whilst reducing overhead costs for companies.

It has been a combination of poor harvests and the extra food requirements of rising populations (especially but not exclusively in the developing countries, which have led to increased over all levels of demand for agricultural and horticultural commodities. Extra global demand for food commodities is a long – term cause of the price variations across the world where as seasonal trends are generally short – term causes of price fluctuations within the contemporary commodity markets.

The surge in global crude oil and petroleum prices had arguably mainly non--economic reasons with the noticeably increased levels of insecurity predominantly caused by the 9 / 11 attacks on the United States and its invasion of Iraq (Klein, 2007 p. 11). Political decisions by the American government in this particular case influenced the leading commodity price variations rather more than seasonal trends in the commodity markets did, with the invasion of Iraq leading to nervousness in the leading stock markets as well as the main commodity markets.

Economists have argued that the price variations can be controlled and seasonal trends made less influential in the commodity markets if they are altered or managed by producers and businesses. In fact commodity producers and businesses selling goods and services can increase their income levels from commodity sales by recreating conditions of scarcity.

The crude oil and the petroleum price rises and variations did not instantly set off a global economic depression. In effect the sharp crude oil price variations after 2002 whilst obviously effecting the commodity markets did not cause undue alarm or panic in the main international stock markets. Global recession did not take place in 2002 arguably due to the relatively easy availability of bank credits as well as loans for individuals, businesses, not to mention national governments. With hindsight it was carelessly given credit, banks loans, and electronically spent money were behaving like the main global commodities that were actually keeping the contemporary global economic system going in the early and the middle years of the 2000s. The price variations and also the seasonal trends inside the contemporary commodity markets during the last decade were not as economically healthy as many might have expected. It was arguably the easy availability of bank credit and vast amounts of risky loans that kept the global economy temporally out of recession despite the commodity market price of crude oil breaking the $100 a barrel barrier.

The international stock markets, the mass media, ordinary consumers, and companies alongside the great majority of national governments at this stage were publicly at least unaware of the grossly unstable situation that the global economic system actually found itself in. Looking at the price variations if casual onlookers as amply demonstrating that there was nothing markedly wrong within the global economy viewed not the seasonal trends in commodity markets in the middle of the 2000s.

The international stock markets were more interested in overvaluing the value of stocks and shares for the majority of the last decade instead of realising that things were about to go wrong in the worst economic disaster after the Wall Street Crash of 1929. The price variations and seasonal trends in commodity markets in the years before the onset of the credit crunch did not appear untoward despite the higher crude oil prices caused by instability in the Middle East particularly.

Indications at present point towards the credit crunch leading to the decreasing of food commodity prices, as people will spend less money on such products due to reduced personal budgets. However food commodity price variations are also strongly influenced by storage and transportation costs, the later of course depending on the price of oil. Evidence also point to the fact non-perishable and non oil / petroleum commodities in the last ten years have seen price variations that have more to do with economic cycles of boom and bust.

The upward movements in the price variations whether or not influenced by seasonal trends came to a largely unexpected and also unpredicted slump in global levels of demand quickly described by the media, governments and economists as the credit crunch. Although a global economic recession had not been caused by rocketing oil prices price variations inside commodity markets started to decline. A decline due to the consequences of banks and financial institutions reeling in the wake of the sub-prime mortgages crisis in the United States and the collapse of the Northern Rock, Halifax, and Royal Bank of Scotland in the United Kingdom.

Epilogue

Since writing this some 15 years ago some drastic events have taken place. To begin with there

was the Arab Spring that led to civil wars, rebellions and regime change in the Middle East.

Then there was the unexpected vote for Brexit when the UK left the EU eventually in 2019.

Then there has been the Russian invasion of Ukraine in 2022, the continued Chinese threat to

invade Taiwan and the regional instability caused by the Israeli – Palestinian war in Gaza.

For further details on Russia and Ukraine see my 2023 work "Russia, the EU, oil supplies,

regional security and the Ukrainian War, also available on Amazon Kindle.

Not to mention the worst global pandemic since Spanish Influenca in the guise of COVID-19.

Bibliography

Bannock, Baxter, & Davis (2003) The Penguin Dictionary of Economics

Begg D, Fischer S, & Dornbusch R, (2005) Economics 8th edition, McGraw Hill London

Bromley, Mackintosh, Brown, and Wuyts (2004) - Making the International: Economic Interdependence and Political Order, Pluto Press, London

Chaudari K, (2001) Long run prices of primary commodities and oil prices, Applied Economics, Vol 33

Cleaver T, (2002), Understanding the World Economy – 2nd edition, Routledge, London and New York

Dehn J (2000) Commodity Price Uncertainty in Developing Countries, WPS 2000 - 12

Fisk R, (2006) The Great War for Civilisation – the conquest of the Middle East, Harper Perennial, London

Frieden J A, and Lake D A (2000) International Political Economy – Perspectives on Global Power and Wealth. Bedford / St Martin's, Boston & New York

Gilpin R (1987) The Political Economy of International Relations, Princeton University Press, Princeton

Grauer F & Litzenberger R (1979) The Pricing of Commodity Futures, Contracts, Nominal Bonds, and other Risky Assets under Commodity Price uncertainty, The Journal of Finance, Vol XXXIV 1, March 1979

Ison S (2000) Economics, Prentice Hall, London

Klein N (2007) The Shock Doctrine, Penguin, London

Siebert H, (2002), The World Economy – 2nd edition, Routledge, London and New York

Slade M E and Thille H (2004) Commodity Spot Prices: An Exploratory Assessment of Market Structure and Forward Trading Effects

Smith D, (2003) Free Lunch –Easily Digestible Economics, Served on a plate, Profile Books, London

Commodity of the month: Wheat Laura Staples **Friday, 13th March 2009**

Wheat is the second most produced foodstuff in the world after maize. In 2007, adverse weather conditions – both flooding and drought – and low inventories caused a severe shortage, hiking prices to their highest levels in 30 years.

Thrift N, (2005) Knowing Capitalism

Todd E, (2002) After the Empire – the breakdown of the American Order, Constable, London